Contents

Editor's Note
All measurements are in metric and represent an average, unless otherwise stated. Figures for animals represent an average adult.

Published in Great Britain in 1980
by Kingfisher Books Limited
(A Grisewood & Dempsey,
Ward Lock joint company)
116 Baker Street, London W1M 2BB.
© Librairie Hachette, Paris 1978.
© Kingfisher Books Limited 1980

BRITISH LIBRARY CATALOGUING
IN PUBLICATION DATA
Cuisin, Michel
  Animals of the African plains
  – (Nature's hidden world).
  1. Zoology – Africa – Juvenile literature
  I. Title   II. Series
  591.9'6   QL336
ISBN 0 7063 6034 6

Printed and Bound by Dai Nippon Printing Company
(Hong Kong) Limited

Nature's Hidden World
Animals of the African Plains

Edited by Michael Chinery

Written by Michel Cuisin

Illustrated by Alexis Oussenko

Translated by Anne-Marie Moore

KINGFISHER BOOKS
WARD LOCK LIMITED

The Lion

The lion and the tiger are the largest members of the cat family. But the lion is the only really sociable cat. It lives in groups called prides. A pride may contain up to 40 animals, but the typical pride has only about 15 lions. There are usually one or two adult males, six or seven adult females, or lionesses, and a number of cubs. Each pride occupies an area of up to 25 square kilometres, which the males guard against other lions. Lions prefer to live in areas of the plains that are dotted with trees.

Lions are killers, but do not hunt everyday. They need a good meal only two or three times a week and, unless they are hungry, they take no notice of animals grazing only a few metres away. Hunting takes place mainly in the evening and at night. The lionesses do most of the hunting, either on their own or in groups. The males are always on hand for food, however, and they eat first even when the lionesses have made the kill. The lionesses and cubs follow and a pride can reduce a zebra to a skeleton in half an hour. In some areas, the lions also get food by driving hyenas away from their kills. Meals are followed by a long sleep. In fact, lions spend most of the day dozing peacefully under the trees.

The King of Beasts
The male lion probably gets the nickname King of the Beasts from his majestic head and shaggy mane, and his domineering manner. He is certainly the most powerful predator on the plains. But he would not tackle a mature elephant or rhinoceros. Lions were once found over nearly all of Africa, but today they are only common in parts of East Africa.

Length (male): 3 m with tail   Weight (male): 250 kg
Height at shoulder (male): 1 m   Lifespan in wild: 20 years
Female always smaller   Maximum speed: 60 km/h

The lion's main weapons are its enormous canine teeth and its great paws, armed with sharp claws. The male also has a horny spike in the tuft at the tip of his tail.

▲ Lions may hunt on their own or in groups. One group may drive the prey towards another group waiting in ambush in the long grass.

▼ In some parts of East Africa, the lionesses and cubs rest in the branches of trees. They are all very friendly and frequently snuggle up to each other and play together.

▼ A lioness gives birth to up to five cubs with speckled coats. She suckles them for about eight months, during which time the speckles gradually disappear.

The African Elephant

The African elephant is the largest of all land-living animals. Individuals can reach a height of four metres at the shoulder and a weight of seven tonnes. When charging, this giant can race along at up to 40 kilometres an hour.

The elephant's tusks spring from the upper jaw. The longest ever recorded were 333 centimetres long and the heaviest weighed 101 kilogrammes. Apart from its tusks, the elephant has only four teeth at any one time. Each of these great molars, or cheek teeth, is about 30 centimetres long and 7 centimetres wide. Even so, the teeth wear away with the constant grinding of twigs and leaves, and the elephant has six sets of them during its life-time.

The elephant has an enormous appetite. It eats up to 400 kilogrammes of grass, leaves, bark and branches each day, often pushing down trees to reach the leaves. The elephant uses its trunk to gather food and push it into its mouth.

Too Many Elephants?

The African elephant once roamed over nearly all of Africa south of the Sahara Desert. But it has been exterminated in many areas, mainly for the ivory of its tusks. Most elephants now live in the national parks of East Africa. The parks are vast, but elephants tend to congregate in small areas. When they become too numerous and damage the vegetation, it is sometimes necessary to cull some of the animals – always the weaker ones. There are about 300,000 elephants on the plains at present. A smaller race lives in the dense forests of West Africa.

Length (with trunk): 6–7.5 m
Height at shoulder: 4 m max.
Female always smaller
Weight: 7 tonnes
Lifespan in wild: 80 years max.

▲ Elephants love water and drink about 180 litres each day. They suck it up into the trunk and then squirt it into their mouths. Elephants also love to bathe and to splash water over themselves (below). They bathe in mud as well as in water and their skins are often caked with mud. When elephants become too numerous, they can destroy vast areas of savanna by breaking down the trees (above right).

The elephant's trunk is made of the nose and upper lip. It is immensely strong, but can also pick up tiny objects with care. Elephants have varying number of nails on their feet.

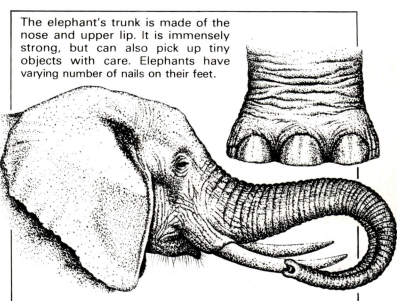

▼ The new-born elephant is up to one metre high and weighs about 120 kilogrammes. It sucks with its mouth.

The Gnu or Wildebeeste

The gnu is one of the strangest of Africa's antelopes. Its hindquarters are slim and elegant like those of most antelopes, but the head and shoulders are large and heavy.

There are two species of gnu – the white-tailed and the black-tailed. The white-tailed gnu has been slaughtered in huge numbers and now lives only in a few game reserves in South Africa. The black-tailed gnu occurs all over southern and East Africa and is one of the commonest of all antelopes. It is also called the brindled gnu, or wildebeeste.

Migrating Herds

The wildebeeste is a very sociable creature. It roams the plains in large or small herds which have no real leaders. The East African animals usually migrate at the beginning of the dry season. The herds come together on the last patches of green pasture and eventually thousands of animals set off westwards in search of fresh grazing. Adult males gather harems of females around them at this time, and the animals mate during the migration. They stay in the damper lands in the west for about three months, and then head eastwards again.

During this return journey the young are born, just in time to make use of the fresh grass that grows when the rains fall on the eastern plains. The large herds then break up until it is time to migrate again. Not all wildebeeste migrate, however. The herds living in wetter regions do not need to go in search of food, for the grass grows well throughout the year.

Length: 2 m (+ tail up to 1 m)
Weight: 150–260 kg
Height at shoulder: 1·3 m
Lifespan in wild: 20 years (male), 11 years (female)

▲ During the breeding season, the males fight with each other to defend a group of females. Horns clash noisily, often for hours, until one male retreats. One male may round up 50 females, but more often two or three males share 100 or more females and fight off rival males.

▼ Lions, hyenas and hunting dogs are the gnu's main enemies. Here, a pair of lionesses stalk a gnu as it grazes. When they begin the chase, the predators separate a gnu from the rest of the herd. Then, as soon as they are near enough, they leap on it and stab it in the neck or throat.

▲ Young gnus, called calves, can stand only ten minutes after birth and they can run soon after that. This is essential if they are to keep up with the herd and avoid their enemies.

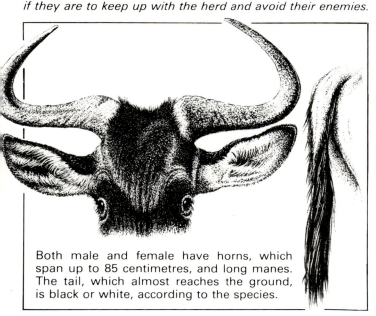

Both male and female have horns, which span up to 85 centimetres, and long manes. The tail, which almost reaches the ground, is black or white, according to the species.

The Baboon

Five species of baboon live on the African plains. They are the largest of the African monkeys and are powerfully built, rather like large dogs. Their heads and long, canine teeth certainly resemble those of some dogs. The three most common species are the chacma baboon of South Africa, the yellow baboon of the eastern and central regions, and the olive baboon of the grasslands to the north of the equator.

Baboons roam the plains in groups of 30 or more – sometimes as many as 100. They feed mainly on grasses, fruit, seeds and roots, but eat large numbers of insects as well, and occasionally kill small birds and mammals. At night, the baboons take to the trees to sleep. Here they are safe from the lions, although a lion would not necessarily get the better of a baboon.

A male baboon is very aggressive and with its enormous teeth can inflict severe damage even on a lion. The baboon often has only to open its mouth and display its teeth to frighten a lion or leopard.

Baboon Hierarchy

The baboon group, known as a troop, is ruled and led by one or more full grown males. All the males have a definite position in the society. A low-ranking male soon learns to step aside when a senior animal comes along. The females have no permanent rank order, but all are lower down the scale than the males. There is very little squabbling in the troop, because each animal knows its place. In fact, the baboons are generally very friendly towards each other. They spend several hours each day grooming (inspecting each other's fur). The leading males are given extra special attention in this respect and the grooming behaviour helps to maintain friendly relations within the troop.

Length: 85 cm (+ 45 cm tail)   Weight: 17–35 kg
Height at shoulder: 65 cm   Lifespan: 10 years
(These figures are for the chacma baboon: other grassland species are similar)

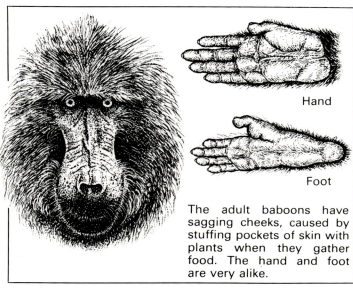

Hand

Foot

The adult baboons have sagging cheeks, caused by stuffing pockets of skin with plants when they gather food. The hand and foot are very alike.

▲ When on the move, the baboons adopt a strict formation. The ruling males, together with the females and young, travel in the middle of the troop. The lower-ranking males are on the outside to defend the troop if necessary.

▼ On rare occasions fighting breaks out among the male baboons, but the dominant male soon puts a stop to it, before any real damage is done to any of the animals.

▼ Baby baboons have to travel with their mothers soon after they are born. Older youngsters ride on their mothers' backs.

Grant's Gazelle

More than 70 different kinds of antelope inhabit the grasslands and forests of Africa. Eleven of them are known as gazelles. They are by no means the smallest of the antelopes, but they are extremely dainty, slim and beautifully proportioned. There are conspicuous dark markings on the face and the coat is usually tawny on the back and white underneath. A dark stripe often runs along the flank. The patterning helps to identify the different species. The horns of the males are strongly ringed and often beautifully curved. Females have smaller, straighter horns.

Grant's gazelle is one of the larger gazelles, with longer horns than the other species. It lives on the drier grasslands of East Africa and, like all gazelles, it avoids dense vegetation. It relies on its speed and agility to escape from lions and other enemies. Grant's gazelle feeds on grasses and low-growing bushes, but it rarely needs to drink.

Herds and Territories

Gazelles are not always as gentle as their elegant appearance might suggest. In fact, the male gazelle fiercely defends a territory measuring up to two kilometres in diameter. Within this territory he lives with his harem of females and their young – a total of up to 30 animals. The male immediately attacks any other mature male which dares to trespass.

Baby Grant's gazelles can stand when only 20 minutes old, but they spend their first days hiding in long grass. Their mothers come to suckle them regularly. Young males leave the group when they grow up and live in bachelor herds until they acquire harems of their own.

Length: 1·4 – 1·8 m
Height at shoulder: 75 – 85 cm
Females smaller

Weight: 45 – 75 kg
Lifespan in captivity: 8 years

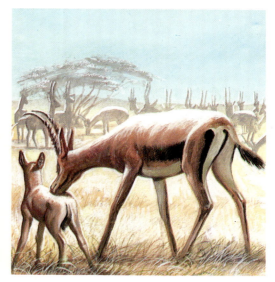

▲ The Grant's gazelle gives birth to her baby in long grass and leaves it there while she feeds. She removes its droppings and keeps it clean so that predators do not smell it.

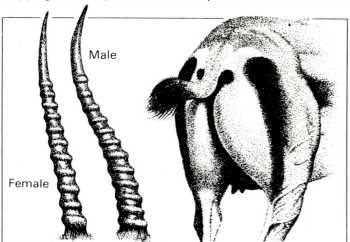

Male horns are up to 75 centimetres long. Female horns are straighter. The distinctive rump pattern identifies Grant's gazelle.

▲ Young gazelles are attacked by lions and other enemies on the ground and also by birds of prey, such as this vulture.

▼ Fighting males often get their horns locked together by the prominent rings and grooves, but the animals are rarely hurt. The weaker male eventually gives up and trots away.

The Secretary Bird

This strange, long-legged bird is found mainly in East and southern Africa. It gets its name from the long plumes that stick out from the back of its head. They are thought to resemble the quill pens that clerks and secretaries once used to put behind their ears.

The secretary bird is a bird of prey and is thus related to the hawks and eagles. But it has different habits from other birds of prey. It spends most of its time strutting over the grasslands and catching a variety of small animals. Secretary birds hunt in pairs over an area of about 60 square kilometres. The grass in this area must be no more than about 50 centimetres high if the birds are to hunt successfully. The secretary bird is also known as the serpent-eater because it readily eats snakes. But these reptiles form only a small percentage of the bird's food. Insects and small rodents are a much more important part of the secretary bird's diet.

Intruders Beware

As they strut through their territories in the daytime, secretary birds are always on the look-out for intruders of the same species. If such an intruder is noticed, the resident bird leaps at it in a frenzied attack. It strikes the trespasser with its feet, throwing its body into extraordinary contortions. The usual result is that the trespasser slinks away.

Although the secretary bird spends most of its life on the ground, it can fly when necessary. In the mating season, the bird soars high into the air and performs breath-taking dives. It spends the night perched in the trees with its legs doubled awkwardly under its body.

Height (male): 1·2 m
Female smaller

Wingspan: 2·1 m
Lifespan: Unknown

16

▲ This secretary bird has caught a snake. It kills it by trampling it under-foot and hammering it with its powerful beak. The bird's long wing feathers keep off any possible strike by the snake. When dead, the snake is usually swallowed whole. The bird also eats lizards and scorpions but its main food consists of rodents, locusts and grasshoppers.

▼ Like many other savanna birds, the secretary bird gathers large amounts of food around bush fires, which force huge numbers of insects and other animals into the open.

The secretary bird's crest consists of about 20 grey and black feathers. Unlike other birds of prey, it cannot grasp with its toes.

▼ The nest is built in a thorny tree. Two or three birds hatch, but the adults rarely rear more than two of them to maturity. At least one chick usually starves to death.

The Cheetah

With a running speed of 80 kilometres an hour, the cheetah is certainly the fastest animal on four legs. Some individuals have even been timed at more than 115 kilometres an hour, covering several metres with each bound. The cheetah's acceleration is even more remarkable – from a standing start it can reach 72 kilometres an hour in two seconds. The cheetah has little stamina, however, and cannot run at full speed for more than about 400 metres.

A Feline Sprinter

The cheetah is a member of the cat family, but it differs from other cats in several ways. Its claws cannot be pulled back into the paws as in other cats and they provide extra grip while sprinting. Its long, wiry legs, slim body and small head are also all modifications for speed. The cheetah hunts by day – unlike most other cats. Gazelles and other small antelopes are its main prey. While the leopard stalks as close as it can to its prey, the cheetah relies on speed when it hunts. It eyes prey from a distance, then creeps slowly towards it, stopping every now and then and 'freezing' if the prey looks up. If it comes within 50 metres of its target, the cheetah breaks into a sprint and very often makes a kill. But gazelles are fast runners as well and they have more stamina than the cheetah. Given a start of more than 50 metres, adult gazelles usually outrun it.

Cheetahs once lived on the open plains all over Africa and southern Asia. But they have been hunted out of existence in many areas and are now common only in parts of East Africa.

Length: 1·3 m (+ 75 cm tail)   *Weight: 50–55 kg*
Height at shoulder: 80–90 cm   *Lifespan: Unknown*

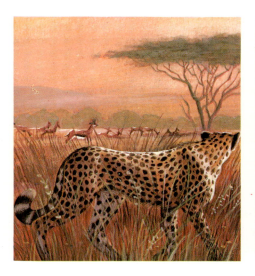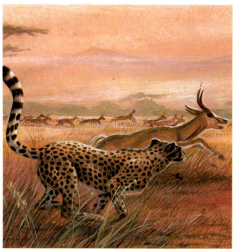

▲ The cheetah hunts early in the morning and late in the afternoon, when it is not too hot. Prey is brought down by the rump or hind legs and killed with a bite on the neck.

The cheetah is easily identified by the black lines down its face. Its long tail is used as a counterbalance when running at speed. The cheetah is hunted for its skin.

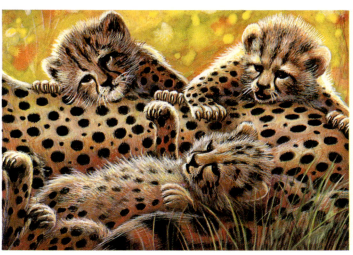

▲ There are two or three baby cheetahs in a litter. They are very playful and start hunting at about seven months.

▼ The cheetah's most common victims are Grant's and Thomson's gazelles. It also catches other antelopes, hares and even birds, such as this great bustard. After a hard chase, the cheetah has to get its breath back before eating.

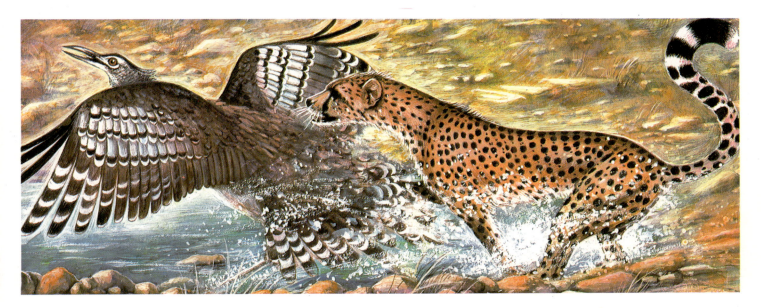

The Spotted Hyena

Three species of hyena live in Africa – the striped hyena, the brown hyena and the spotted hyena. They all have large heads and coarse coats and their hunchback bodies slope down distinctively from the shoulders to the rump.

The spotted hyena has exceptionally powerful jaws and teeth. It can crush bones which all the other carnivores, including the lion, have to leave. For a long time, the hyena was thought of as a typical scavenger, unable to capture its own food and content to clear up dead bodies and scraps left by other flesh-eaters. The hyena does eat carrion, but generally only as a daytime snack. At night it joins forces with other hyenas and becomes a very efficient hunter. Packs of hyenas run down such animals as wildebeeste, zebras and gazelles. They even attack lion cubs and baby elephants, and in some places drive lions and cheetahs from their kill. But elsewhere the roles may be reversed with lions robbing hyenas.

Howls in the Night

Spotted hyenas are larger than the other African species and can be found in most grassland areas to the south of the Sahara. They live in clans of up to 100 animals. Each clan is ruled by a female. The members of a clan are generally very friendly towards each other, but they fight other hyenas that wander into their territory. When an intruder is noticed, the hyenas become very excited. Their manes bristle and the night air is filled with spine-chilling howls of laughter. Hyenas make the same dreadful din during the breeding season and there is always much rowdy squabbling while they eat.

Length: 1·3–1·6 m (+ 30 cm tail)
Weight: 45–85 kg
Height at shoulder: 75–90 cm
Lifespan in wild: 25 years

▲ Hyenas usually hunt in the evenings or at night and tirelessly chase their prey over long distances. But they are not always successful: here a lion hijacks their target and makes the kill.

▼ Although mammals are its main prey, the spotted hyena sometimes creeps along the edges of lakes and catches young flamingoes standing in the water. It also eats insects and village rubbish.

The spotted hyena has a rather shaggy coat. It has good hearing, sharp eyesight and an excellent sense of smell.

▼ The female generally gives birth to two furry cubs in a burrow. She suckles them for up to a year until they can hunt.

The Giraffe

The giraffe, with its extraordinary neck, is the tallest living animal. A large male can browse on acacia leaves as much as six metres above the ground. Despite its great length, the giraffe's neck has exactly the same number of vertebrae as a human neck, or even the neck of a mouse – just seven bones. They are, of course, large bones. A strong heart is needed to pump the blood to the top of this long neck and the giraffe's heart is very large – 60 centimetres long and up to 11 kilogrammes in weight.

Giraffes are found today mainly in eastern and southern Africa, with a few small populations on the plains of West Africa. There are eight different races, each with a different pattern of markings. The giraffes live in small, loosely-organized herds in areas where there are enough trees to feed them. But they avoid dense forests. Old males are often solitary, and young males tend to form bachelor clubs until they reach breeding age.

Timid Giants

Although giraffes can make a variety of bleating and grunting noises, they are very quiet animals. In zoos they hardly ever make sounds. They also have a quiet nature and keep very much to themselves. In the wild they avoid other animals and prefer to flee from their enemies than to fight. The giraffes fight when necessary, however, and can use their powerful legs and hooves to inflict serious and often fatal injuries on any attacker. Apart from people, lions are their only real enemies, although hyenas and leopards occasionally kill young giraffes.

Mating takes place at any time of the year and the males often fight among themselves for the right to mate with a female. The fights may also decide who leads the male herds. Generally these skirmishes are not very serious. Two males swing their long necks at each other and rub their heads together. This is called 'necking'. Real fighting is much more dramatic with the giraffes wielding their bony heads like clubs. But again they rarely injure each other.

Weight: 1250 kg
Height at shoulder: 3–3·75 m
Total height: 6·1 m maximum
(female smaller)
Lifespan in captivity: 28 years

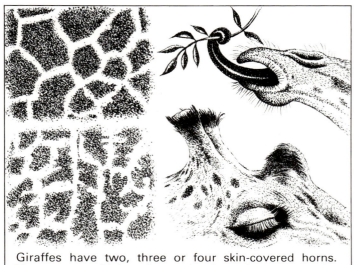

Giraffes have two, three or four skin-covered horns. The tongue, which gathers twigs from the trees, can be up to 40 centimetres long. The coat pattern varies.

▲ Acacia leaves and shoots are the giraffe's main food. The animal feeds by night and by day and chews the cud while standing or walking slowly. It usually runs away from a lion.

▼ In order to drink, the giraffe has to spread its front legs wide apart. But it can go for long periods without water.

▼ The baby giraffe is about 1·6 metres tall when it is born. It begins to eat leaves after two weeks and may leave its mother at six weeks.

The Red-Billed Hornbill

There are about 45 species of hornbill in Africa and Asia. Most live in the forests. But the red-billed hornbill, shown on these pages, prefers the forest edge and the tree-dotted savanna. It is one of the smallest hornbills and can be found in many places south of the Sahara. The bird displays great agility in the trees, but it hops rather awkwardly when hunting on the ground. Ants, termites and young locusts form the bulk of its diet, together with some fruits and seeds. The hornbill's short, rounded wings prevent it from flying quickly. When it does fly, it usually flaps its wings rapidly for a few seconds and then glides for some distance.

Self-Imprisonment
Most hornbills go to extraordinary lengths to protect their eggs and young. The nesting female generally walls herself up in a tree trunk leaving just a small hole through which her mate can feed her. First the male and female select a suitable tree hole and furnish it with small twigs and leaves. Then the female begins to close up the entrance from the inside. She uses mud, clay and dung brought to her by the male, and she may also use saliva and her own droppings. The material sets rock hard and the wall is a very effective defence against all enemies. Up to five eggs are laid, sometimes before the wall is complete.

While she is walled in the tree trunk, the female takes the opportunity to renew most of her feathers. For a short time, she has no wing feathers and she would be quite helpless if the nest were broken open. The male feeds his mate throughout the incubation period and also brings the young birds' food for the first few weeks. The female then breaks out of her prison and helps to collect food for the youngsters until they are ready to leave the nest themselves. The young birds wall themselves in again once their mother has left.

Length: 44 cm
Weight: 135–185 g
Incubation period: 1 month

▲ The red-billed hornbill often nests in old woodpecker holes. The female stocks the cavity with twigs and leaves, then begins to close up the entrance from the inside. Finally the hole is just wide enough for the male's beak.

The beak is up to 8·5 centimetres long. The legs of this species are short. Ground-living species have longer legs.

▲ The mother leaves the nest about three weeks before the young and helps the male to feed them with insects and small fruits. The young have huge appetites by this time.

▼ The female hornbill can plug the nest entrance with her horny beak and fight off enemies, such as this tree snake.

The Black Rhinoceros

The black rhinoceros has a reputation for being aggressive and unpredictable: sometimes it will charge furiously when disturbed, while at other times it stands and stares or simply trots away. The explanation lies in the animal's poor eyesight and its reliance on its senses of smell and hearing. The rhinoceros probably sees a man 30 metres away as just a vague shadow and takes no notice of him. But if disturbed by a sound and able to smell a human intruder, the rhinoceros may well charge. Even then the charge may not be a serious attack. The rhinoceros may simply want to investigate further. But it is as well to get out of its way. Although it looks rather clumsy, the rhinoceros is both speedy and agile and it can wheel around almost on the spot.

The black rhinoceros can be found over much of southern and eastern Africa. But its numbers are falling as a result of hunting and there may be only about 12,000 left. The rhinoceros feeds mainly on shrubs, including very spiny ones. It pulls down leaves and branches with its hooked snout.

White and Black Equal Grey
The other African rhinoceros is the white rhinoceros. But it is not white any more than the black rhinoceros is black. Both animals are grey. The white rhinoceros is a grazing animal and it has a very wide, square snout. Its name probably comes from a Dutch word meaning 'wide'. The white rhinoceros is a much larger and rarer animal than the black. It is also more peaceful and more sociable. It lives in small herds, whereas the grumpy black rhino generally lives alone.

Length: 3·6 m (+ 70 cm tail) *Weight: 1–2 tonnes*
Height at shoulder: 1·5 m *Lifespan in captivity: 50 years*

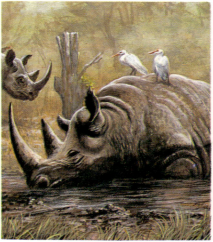

▲ Tick birds (brown) often perch on the rhinoceros's back. They eat the ticks that suck the rhino's blood, and also fly up, warning the rhinoceros of danger. Cattle egrets (white) also perch on its back and catch insects disturbed by the rhino.

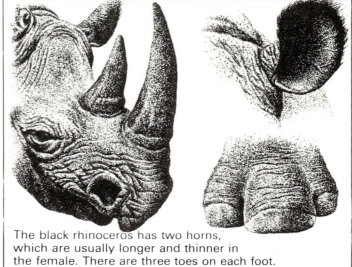

▲ The young rhino weighs about 40 kilogrammes at birth. It is hornless at first and is suckled for about 18 months.

▼ A charging rhinoceros can move at 45 kilometres an hour. It loves to wallow in swamps and plaster its nearly hairless body with mud. The mud protects it from insect bites.

The black rhinoceros has two horns, which are usually longer and thinner in the female. There are three toes on each foot.

Termites

Countless millions of insects live on the African plains. Most numerous are the termites, ants and the locusts. The termites live in large colonies which are 'ruled' by a king and a queen. There may be over one million termites in a single colony. Each termite belongs to one of several different forms, or castes, and does a particular job for the good of the whole colony. Workers, for example, collect food and soldiers guard the nest. The queen lays the eggs. Her whole body becomes a vast 'egg factory' and she looks like a pale sausage with her tiny head and legs at one end. At certain times she lays thousands of eggs each day. The record is held by a species from Natal which produces up to 40,000 eggs in 24 hours. Up to 12 centimetres long and 2·5 centimetres in diameter, she is about 2400 times the size of the workers who look after her.

Air-Conditioned Cities

Many termites live entirely under the ground. But several savanna species raise huge tower-like nests. The tallest mounds are about 6 metres high and the largest ever found was over 20 metres across. The walls of these great nests are made of earth, cemented with the insects' droppings and saliva. They may be 60 centimetres thick and are iron-hard.

Inside the nest there is a maze of tunnels and chambers in which the worker termites rear their younger brothers and sisters and store the food. Many of the savanna termites feed on seeds and grasses, but others actually grow their own food in the form of fungi. This is cultivated on beds of droppings and chewed grass. Elaborate tunnel systems make sure that air circulates through the nest and keeps the fungus gardens and the living quarters at the right temperature and humidity (level of moisture).

Most termites emerge only at night. But even then they are rarely seen, for they usually build covered walks between their nests and food-collecting grounds. The workers are all wingless, but swarms of winged termites emerge at certain times. These are the new kings and queens setting out on their mating flights.

Length of soldier: up to 2 cm
Length of worker: 1–10 mm
(size varies with species)
Lifespan of queen: several decades
Lifespan of worker: 2–4 years

▼ *Thousands of winged termites emerge at mating time, but few escape the kites, bee-eaters and other birds. Other termite-eating animals include the aardvark and the pangolin – mammals that break open the mounds with their claws.*

▲ *The king and queen live in a royal chamber which is much larger than the others. They have wings for their mating flight, but they break them off afterwards. Once the queen's body begins to swell, she does nothing but lay eggs.*

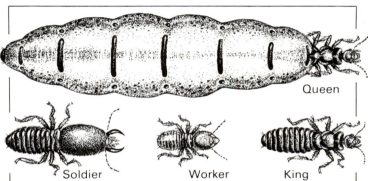

The queen dwarfs the other termite castes. Soldiers defend the colony with their large jaws but, like the king and queen, they have to be fed by workers. Termites are usually very pale and are often called white ants.

▼ *The queen can hardly move and is always surrounded by workers who feed and clean her, and care for her eggs.*

The Zebra

The zebra is a cousin of the horse and the only large mammal with a black and white coat. You might think that the striped pattern makes the animal more conspicuous, but on the plains it does just the opposite. The pattern breaks up the animals' outlines, making it difficult to pick them out when they are some distance away – especially for the lion, which probably sees everything in black and white.

There are three species of zebra. Grevy's zebra lives in Ethiopia and neighbouring areas. It is the largest species and has no stripes on its belly. The mountain zebra is the smallest. It lives only in southern and south-western Africa. Burchell's zebra is the commonest species. It occupies large parts of eastern and central Africa. They are all hardy animals and thrive on tough plants.

Lions and hyenas are the zebra's main enemies, but the zebra can usually out-run them. If it is caught, it can defend itself well with its hooves.

Herds of Harems

Herds containing hundreds of zebras roam the plains. These herds actually consist of large numbers of distinct family units called harems. Each harem is made up of an adult male, or stallion, together with a few females and their young – a total of about 15 animals. The stallion and his mares form a very stable unit. If he becomes weak or dies, the group stays together and is adopted by a new stallion. Young males leave the harem when they are about two years old and live in bachelor herds for a while. Some young females stay in the harem, but most are attracted away by bachelor males about to form their own harems. The herds often mingle with other savanna animals, such as gnus and ostriches.

Length: 2·2 m (+ 75 cm tail)
Weight: 225–400 kg (according to species)
Height at shoulder: 1·2–1·4 m (according to species)
Lifespan in wild: Up to 40 years

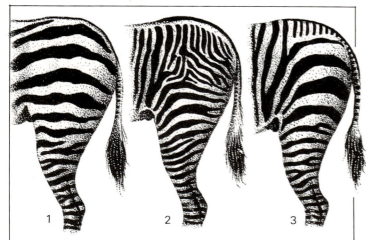

Burchell's zebra (1) has broadly-spaced stripes. Grevy's zebra (2) has narrower stripes (and very large ears). The mountain zebra (3) has a grid-iron pattern on its rump.

▼ *Baby zebras are born all the year round. They weigh up to 35 kilogrammes at birth and are suckled for six months.*

▲ *Zebras do not appear to suffer from drought as much as some savanna animals. They are content to graze on tough grass stems, but they do not move far from the water holes. When alarmed, they warn the herd with a loud yelp or bark.*

▼ *Zebra stallions fight other males that break into the harem to steal the females. They kick and bite fiercely.*

The Ostrich

The ostrich is the world's largest living bird. The males, which are a little larger than the females, can reach heights of over two metres and weights of 150 kilogrammes. Not surprisingly this huge bird cannot fly. Its wings are very small and its feathers are fluffy and quite unsuited for flight. The bird's body, with its long powerful legs, has been developed for speed over the ground. It can trot along happily at 45 kilometres an hour and sprint at over 65 kilometres an hour, covering two metres with one stride.

Ostriches were once common all over the grasslands and semi-deserts of Africa and Arabia. But thousands were killed for their feathers. Large numbers of ostriches are now found only in East Africa. In some places, the birds are reared on ranches and their feathers are plucked every now and then.

A Varied Diet

Ostriches are omnivorous birds, which means that they eat almost anything. In captivity, they swallow sticks, jewellery, buttons and golf balls – almost anything that can be swallowed. Their diet in the wild is not quite so unusual, but nevertheless it is very varied. Seeds, leaves and fruit make up the bulk of the ostriches' food, but they also eat insects, lizards and other small animals. Berries and succulent plants provide them with water in dry regions and the birds also gulp down sand and gravel to help them grind up their food.

Ostriches often live in large herds, but they split up into family groups during the rainy season. A male adopts a territory away from its feeding grounds. His head and neck then turn red which helps him to attract one or more females to lay their eggs in a hollow. He also puts on a splendid courtship dance, during which he sits down and sways from side to side with his wings open. This encourages the females to mate with him. The male and one hen then look after as many as 30 eggs, each weighing as much as one kilogramme.

Height: 2·4 m maximum
Weight: 70–150 kg
(males much heavier than females)
Incubation period: 6 weeks

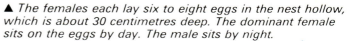
▲ *The females each lay six to eight eggs in the nest hollow, which is about 30 centimetres deep. The dominant female sits on the eggs by day. The male sits by night.*

▼ *Ostrich eggs are up to 17 centimetres long. The downy chicks can run as soon as they hatch. They follow the adults after one or two days.*

The ostrich is the only living bird with just two toes. It uses its large eyes to spot danger from afar. Its fluffy feathers were once very popular for ladies' hats.

▼ *The ostrich's height gives it a good view over the plains. When it sees a lion or other enemy, it runs away and thus warns other animals.*

The Leopard

As an athlete and a gymnast, the leopard has few rivals in the animal world. It can leap six to eight metres in one bound, climb trees with ease and walk along slender branches with the confidence of a tight-rope walker. The leopard often waits high in a tree for prey to walk below, and then, with one well-timed leap, it brings the victim crashing to the ground. The leopard has tremendous strength as well and can even drag an animal twice its own weight into a tree. The leopard only has difficulty when pursuing prey. It does not have much staying power and gives up the chase after about 100 metres. It relies on stealth and agility to capture the antelopes and other animals on which it feeds.

Most of the leopard's hunting is done at dusk and dawn, when its sleek, dappled coat provides excellent camouflage. The leopard selects a suitable victim, crouches as low as possible and creeps silently forward, without ever taking its eyes off the target.

When it is within range, the leopard either rushes at its prey or springs on it with one great bound. Claws and teeth quickly kill the victim.

A Widespread Hunter

The leopard is the most widely distributed of all the big cats. It can be found nearly all over Africa and throughout most of southern Asia. It inhabits thick forest, mountain and near-desert as well as the savanna. The coat pattern varies from place to place and in the tropical forests some of the leopards are completely black. They are called black panthers. Leopards are much rarer today than they were in the past because so many have been killed for their beautiful coats.

Length: 1·3 m (+ 90 cm tail)
Weight: 40–80 kg (males much heavier than females)
Height at shoulder: 70 cm
Lifespan in captivity: 21 years

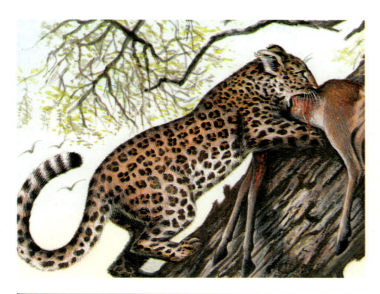

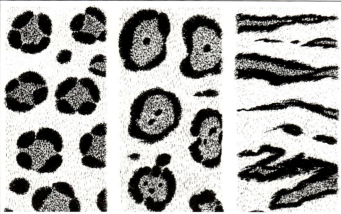

The leopard's spots (left) form rosettes, but there are no central spots as there are in the American jaguar (centre). The cheetah's spots do not form rosettes (see page 18), while the American ocelot has a mixture of spots and stripes (right).

▲ A leopard can eat only a few kilogrammes of meat at a sitting. Antelopes and other larger prey are partly eaten and the rest is often carried high into a tree to store for another day. The leopard eats birds, pigs, rodents, jackals and even insects.

▼ Two or three baby leopards are born in a cave or similar shelter. They stay with their mother for about two years.

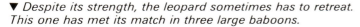

▼ Despite its strength, the leopard sometimes has to retreat. This one has met its match in three large baboons.

The Ratel or Honey Badger

The honey badger, or ratel, inhabits the African forest as well as the plains and it can be found in areas throughout South-West Asia to India. It is called the honey badger because of its love for honey. It often finds this food in a most extraordinary manner – through the help of a small bird called a honey-guide.

Africans tell many stories about the strange relationship between the honey-guide and the ratel, but the details are not always clear. It seems that when the honey-guide sees a ratel, it becomes very excited and, attracted by the noise, the ratel follows it and is led to a bees' nest. The bird watches silently as the ratel breaks open the nest and greedily gulps down the honey and grubs, scattering fragments of wax combs. Then, when the ratel has finished, the honey-guide snaps up the pieces of wax. The association between these animals is strange because they do not really need each other's help. Both can find and enter bees' nests on their own.

The ratel also feeds on a wide variety of foods apart from honey. Rodents, birds, insects and plants make up most of its diet but it also eats scorpions and snakes. Its tough skin and dense fur protect it from their stings and fangs until they are bitten to death.

A Fearless Fighter

Although it feeds mainly on small animals, the honey badger is a ferocious creature and extremely strong for its size. It has no hesitation in attacking animals much larger than itself and has been known to attack a buffalo with its powerful teeth. One ratel tackled and killed a python over three metres long. The honey badger's strong claws also allow it to tunnel easily. It can dig itself into very hard ground in less than ten minutes.

Length: 75 cm (+ 25 cm tail)   Weight: 11 kg
Height at shoulder: 30 cm   Lifespan: Unknown

The front claws are as much as 4·6 centimetres long – twice the length of the hind claws. Strong teeth tear up all kinds of flesh, including carrion.

▲ The honey-guide first attracts the ratel by calling noisily and then leads it to a wild bees' nest. The ratel gorges itself on the honey, with its thick skin and dense fur protecting it from the angry bees.

▼ The ratel will gobble insects as well as attack much larger animals. Its bold black and white pattern is believed to warn other animals to steer clear, especially as the ratel, like the skunk, can spray its enemies with a foul-smelling liquid.

▼ Only two babies are born at a time, in a burrow or a hole in the rocks. They first emerge when about six weeks old and leave their mother after about six months. The animals are usually solitary, but they sometimes hunt in pairs.

Vultures

Vultures are often thought of as greedy unpleasant birds because they eat dead animals, even when the flesh is rotting and smelly. These habits are unattractive to us, but the birds are really playing a very important role by cleaning up the rubbish. Jackals, hyenas, crows, kites and many insects also help to rid the plains of dead animals.

Ten species of vulture live in Africa. With the exception of the Egyptian and bearded vultures, their heads and necks are bare. If they were feathered, they would become matted with blood when the vultures dug into rotting carcasses. The lappet-faced vulture, with a wingspan of about 2·8 metres, is the largest of the African vultures. Other well-known species include Ruppell's vulture, which is common on the northern and eastern grasslands, and the white-backed vulture.

Vultures all have very broad wings and can soar for hours on end as they scan the ground for food. Their eyesight is extremely sharp, and as soon as a vulture spots a carcass, it glides quickly down to feed. It will also come down close to a group of feeding lions, knowing that they always leave a few scraps. Soaring vultures always keep an eye on each other as well. When one drops, its neighbours will come down to investigate.

The Food Queue

Several kinds of vulture may gather round a carcass, but they do not all feed at once. The larger species feed first and the smaller ones take what is left. The Egyptian vulture can only pick the last scraps of flesh from the bones, and this explains why it does not have a bare neck.

Ruppell's vulture (above)
Length: 1 m
Wingspan: 2·2 m
Weight: 5–6 kg
Lifespan: Unknown

▲ Large numbers of vultures quickly gather around a carcass and tear it to pieces. The Egyptian vulture (centre) must wait until its larger cousins have finished. But its narrow beak can scoop small pieces of meat from between the bones.

Vultures have strong, sharp beaks to slash skin and flesh. But they do not actually kill their food, and their talons are rather small and weak.

▲ Ruppell's vulture nests in colonies on steep rock faces. These nests are made of twigs and are used for several years.

▼ The Egyptian vulture can crack ostrich eggs by throwing stones at them. The bird picks up a stone and dashes it against an egg until it breaks. The vulture's rough tongue then laps up the liquid.

The Buffalo

The majestic buffalo, with its great sweeping horns, is often referred to as the Cape buffalo, although it can be found in most parts of Africa south of the Sahara. The buffalo lives in both grassland and forest. The grassland animals, illustrated on these pages, can weigh over 1000 kilogrammes, but the forest ones rarely weigh more than 300 kilogrammes. The forest race was once thought to belong to a different species. Its horns sweep backwards to allow it to move easily through the trees.

A Dangerous Opponent

Despite its weight and size, the buffalo is an agile animal and can trundle along at 20 kilometres an hour for several hundred metres. It is one of the most feared and dangerous of the African game animals because it panics and often stampedes if it is startled. Anything in its way is likely to be trampled or gored to death. Even the lion treats the buffalo with respect, although lions will catch young buffalo that stray from their herds.

While the buffalo herd is grazing, a few of its members look out for any unusual movement. The cattle egrets and ox-peckers which perch on the buffaloes' backs also act as 'watchdogs'. They fly up when anything approaches and so warn the herd. Once alerted, the animals stand their ground and are a match for any lion that dares to attack.

The huge buffalo herds that once roamed the savanna have been greatly reduced by hunting and also by a disease called rinderpest. The animals caught this from cattle brought in by European settlers. Herds of several hundred buffalo can still be seen in some of the game parks, although most herds are much smaller.

Figures for savanna race
Length: 2·2 m (+ 75 cm tail)   *Weight: 1350 kg max.*
Height at shoulder: 1·7 m   *Lifespan in wild: 16–20 years*

▲ The buffalo feeds mainly on grasses, by day and by night. In the middle of the day it seeks shady places in which to rest and chew the cud. The buffalo also needs to drink regularly at a water hole and enjoys wallowing in water.

▼ Cattle egrets are rarely far from the buffalo herds. The birds often perch on the animals' backs and feed on the grasshoppers and other insects disturbed by the buffaloes' hooves. Ox-peckers eat ticks from the buffaloes' skin.

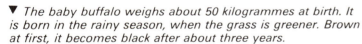

The buffalo is a cloven-hoofed animal like the domestic cow. Each horn may be one metre long. The massive bases of the horns cover the forehead of an adult male and can even protect the animal from a bullet.

▼ The baby buffalo weighs about 50 kilogrammes at birth. It is born in the rainy season, when the grass is greener. Brown at first, it becomes black after about three years.

The Cape Hunting Dog

The Cape hunting dog can be found in most parts of the African plains, although it is most common in eastern areas. It lives and works in packs which are remarkable for the cooperation shown between the individual members.

A pack generally contains between 6 and 20 animals, although some have as many as 60 dogs. The pack ranges over an area of about 2500 square kilometres. The dogs settle in one part of the range when pups are about to be born, but otherwise they wander freely over the whole area.

Small antelopes, such as the gazelles and impala, are the main prey of the hunting dogs, but some packs regularly kill gnus and zebras. The dogs rely on well-organized team-work when hunting and they achieve this through elaborate noisy ceremonies before they start. They wag their tails and lick and kiss each other, gradually building up the excitement. Then they all move off at a trot, slowing down when they find a herd of antelope. When the antelope begin to run, the dogs speed after them at up to 50 kilometres an hour. Each dog picks out a particular antelope to chase. But the dogs watch each other and, as soon as they see that one dog is closing in on its prey, they all turn their attention to the one victim. Racing in from all sides, they quickly bring down the antelope by snapping at its legs and rump. The whole prey can be torn to pieces and eaten in ten minutes.

Food for the Pups

The younger dogs are generally allowed to feed at the kill first and the dogs will hunt again if there is not enough food to go round. If there are pups in the den, the dogs never forget to take food back for them and for the adults who stay behind to guard them.

It was thought that all the dogs in a pack had equal rank, because during the hunt there is no obvious leader. Recent studies, however, have shown that a pack does have 'rulers'. But as the animals are so friendly towards each other, it is very hard to determine who they are.

Length: 1 m (+ 40 cm tail)
Height at shoulder: 65 cm
Weight: 27–35 kg
Lifespan in wild: 10–12 years

▲ Hunting dogs hunt mainly at dawn and late in the afternoon. Although noisy before they start, they chase in silence. If the prey veers off to one side, dogs from the back of the pack may cut across and head it off. The victim is quickly torn to pieces.

The ears are large and play an important part in tracking down prey. Coat patterns vary tremendously.

▲ The female has up to ten pups at a time. Before they are big enough to go on the hunt, they are fed with partly-digested meat by the returning adults, not necessarily their mother.

▼ Whenever they meet, the members of a pack greet each other by 'kissing' and tail-wagging. Such greetings may last five minutes and they help to maintain the solidarity of the pack. There are rarely any squabbles between members.

Savanna-Sea of Grass

About one-third of Africa's land surface – about ten million square kilometres – is covered by open grassy plains known as savanna. These grasslands cover most of southern and eastern Africa and run in a wide band right across the continent between the Sahara and the tropical forests around the Equator.

Rainfall over this vast area tends to be seasonal and is not usually enough to support the growth of trees. Thorny umbrella-shaped acacia trees and giant baobab trees grow in scattered clumps in some areas. They can resist long periods of drought and their tough trunks can survive the frequent fires that sweep across the land in the dry season. But these trees never become numerous because the seedlings are either killed off in the fires or munched by animals. Grasses can resist drought, recover from fire and regrow after being cropped by animals. Therefore they are the dominant plants of the savanna.

Several kinds of savanna can be recognized. The damper areas around the tropical forests support Guinean savanna with long grass and fairly large numbers of trees. At the other end of the scale there is the shrubby savanna bordering the deserts. Here the dry season lasts for at least eight months and the vegetation consists of short grasses and thorny bushes. Between these two extremes comes the grassy savanna – the home of the various animals described in this book.

Dwarfs and Giants

The savanna's sea of grasses and scattered trees provides food for an immense population of animals, both large and small. Beetles, grasshoppers, ants, termites and many other insects nibble the grasses in their millions. Although tiny, these creatures play a major role in savanna life. They are snapped up by lizards and birds and these in turn are eaten by snakes and many carnivorous mammals. But it is the large mammals that dominate the African plains. More than 40 kinds of large browsing and grazing mammals live there as well as a variety of smaller antelopes.

Despite their numbers, the plant-eaters run no risk of exhausting their food supplies under normal circumstances because they all have slightly different feeding habits. Zebra, for example eat the tough tops of grasses, wildebeeste the leafy centres, and gazelles the leaves and shoots at ground level. The taller antelopes tend to browse on the scattered trees and shrubs, leaving the shorter plants for the smaller species, while the giraffes crop leaves out of the reach of all. Seasonal migrations also help to maintain food supplies because the grasses can recover while the herds are feeding in other areas.

Hunters and the Hunted

Preying on the herds of plant-eaters are some savage carnivores. These include the large cats – the lion, the leopard and the cheetah – the hyenas and the hunting dogs. There are few hiding places on the plains and the herbivores rely mainly on speed and stamina to avoid being caught. Their legs are modified for speed with powerful muscles bunched at the top to swing the legs efficiently. The animals run on the tips of their toes which increases the length of the stride and therefore the animal's speed. Keen sight, good hearing and the habit of roaming in herds also improves their safety. Each individual is on the alert for danger, and predators are often confused when facing large numbers of prey. When they do make a kill, it is usually a weaker member of the herd. The stronger ones escape and maintain their herds in good condition.

GREYSCALE

BIN TRAVELER FORM

Cut By **Melvis L. # 02**   Qty **32**   Date **03/26/26**

Scanned By _____ Qty _____ Date _____

Scanned Batch ID's

_____ _____ _____

Notes / Exception